Original title:
Ripe with Joy

Copyright © 2025 Creative Arts Management OÜ
All rights reserved.

Author: Colin Leclair
ISBN HARDBACK: 978-1-80586-366-3
ISBN PAPERBACK: 978-1-80586-838-5

Moments Illuminated

In the garden of laughter, we dance and we twirl,
With tomatoes that giggle and carrots that swirl.
The bees wear top hats, oh what a delight,
As they buzz along, giggling into the night.

The sun plays a trick, casting shadows so loud,
While cucumbers blush in their leafy green shroud.
A playful wind whispers, 'Let's have some fun!'
As the pumpkins jump high, letting laughter outrun.

Farmer Joe's dog dons a colorful bow,
Chasing after shadows, putting on quite the show.
A dance of the veggies, it's quite the surprise,
With laughter and joy painting smiles in our eyes.

So gather your friends, let the silliness flow,
In a garden where tickles and giggles will grow.
We'll feast on our mishaps, laughter in the air,
In this world full of moments, we find joy everywhere.

Harmonies of Happiness

Singing in the sun, birds take flight,
Bouncing on the grass, it's pure delight.
Cake-flavored clouds, a fluffy array,
We'll dance till the dawn, come what may.

Laughter like bubbles, floating so high,
Jellybean rainbows, oh my, oh my!
Tickle fights breaking the starlit gloom,
Slippers on cats, they twirl and zoom.

Glimmers of Grace

A squirrel on a swing, how silly it seems,
Banana peels hiding in whimsical dreams.
Umbrellas like mushrooms bloom in the park,
Giggling together until it's dark.

Juggling with lemons, oh what a sight,
Chasing our shadows, feeling so light.
Skating on puddles, a slippery run,
Every splash echoes, we're having such fun!

Golden Moments Glimpse

Bouncing like beans, we leap and we hop,
Ice cream mustaches, we can't help but stop.
The sun paints our faces with laughter's sweet tone,
A parade of goofballs, we're never alone.

Monkeys in hats, what a view to behold,
Tickling the funny bone, never gets old.
Wobbling like jelly, we roll on the floor,
Chasing our giggles, we come back for more.

Harvest of Laughter

Pickles and pancakes, oh what a spread,
Laughter erupts, we're all filled with bread.
A dance with the moon, we twirl in the night,
Bananas in pajamas, what a silly sight!

Frisbees like flying saucers in play,
Guffaws fill the air, driving clouds away.
With a grin: 'Who chicken danced?' the crowd roars,
Join us in merriment as joy restores!

Tiny Celebrations

A cupcake slides from my hand,
Landing soft on the ground.
Its sprinkles dance, oh what a sight,
Laughter erupts, joy all around.

The cat wears a hat, looking so grand,
Chasing shadows that flutter and flit.
A balloon floats away in the sun,
We giggle and chase—it's a silly fit.

Laughter in the Valley

In the valley, a picnic unfolds,
Sandwiches flying, the ants cheer.
We toss chips, like confetti galore,
As squirrels dance, they approach with no fear.

A funny hat made of cheese,
Worn by our friend, the jester supreme.
Laughter erupts with each silly pose,
Creating memories that sparkle and beam.

Bridging Hearts

Two friends roll down a grassy hill,
Like tumbleweeds in a joyful spree.
With giggles that burst like bubbles in air,
They land with a thud, wild and free.

Skateboards whiz past, dodging the trees,
With laughter so loud, it echoes the sound.
A pie flies by side, splat! What a glance!
In this mad world, true joy knows no bounds.

Blossoming Dreams

In the garden, a gnome jigs with glee,
Waving at flowers that sway to the beat.
A daisy does a hilarious twirl,
As a bumblebee joins, feel the heat!

Under the sun, we mix up some fun,
With paint on our faces, bright like a show.
With each silly dance, laughter ignites,
In this land of dreams where joy loves to flow.

Fruits of Laughter

In a garden where giggles grow,
Bananas slip and put on a show.
Mangoes bounce with a cheeky grin,
While berries whisper, "Let the fun begin!"

Apples roll, they play tag and race,
Chasing lemons with zest and grace.
Peaches blush, oh what a sight,
As cherries cheer with pure delight!

Abundance in Bloom

Flowers bloom in colors bright,
Turning heads, oh what a sight!
Tulips tease with their playful sway,
Dancing in the sun, come out to play.

Daisies giggle in the breeze,
Tickled by whispers of honeybees.
A sunflower winks with golden cheer,
Spilling laughter as spring draws near.

Harvesting Happiness

Silly squash and jovial beans,
Decorate fields like laughter scenes.
Pumpkins chuckle, round and bold,
Sharing secrets that never get old.

Corn on the cob tells jokes in rows,
As zany zucchinis strike silly poses.
Carrots tap dance in the warm sun,
Harvesting smiles, oh what fun!

Sunlit Whispers

In the sun, the daisies play,
Whispers of silliness light the day.
Butterflies flutter with giggly grace,
Chasing shadows, a playful race.

Kite strings tangle in happy spins,
While grasshoppers jump with silly grins.
Nature chuckles in the bright, warm air,
Sunlit whispers everywhere!

Lush Moments

Sunshine tickles the tops of trees,
Squirrels dance like they own the breeze.
A pineapple smiles, so round and bold,
Telling secrets only fruit can hold.

Berries burst in laughter, a colorful crew,
Grapes gossip softly, as if they knew.
Mangoes swing from branches, in bright display,
While lemons throw parties, in their zesty way.

Radiant Revelries

The cake wobbles in a festive glee,
Frosting whispers jokes, oh so carefree.
Cupcakes wear smiles, sprinkles on top,
They giggle and jiggle, they never stop.

Ice cream cones bobbing, a comical sight,
Scoops of pure laughter, shining so bright.
A parade of flavors, all in a line,
Chanting 'Life is sweet!' with sugar divine.

The Flavor of Freedom

Pickles jump in the jar with flair,
While mustard confesses without a care.
Ketchup chuckles, a splash of cheer,
As buns dance around, spreading good vibes here.

Hot dogs in a relay, racing with zest,
Condiments cheer as they flavor the best.
Freedom tastes like a picnic delight,
With laughter and joy, from morning to night.

Joyful Abundance

Harmony ripens in an orchard bright,
Where apples wear smiles, oh what a sight!
Peaches tell tales of summers gone by,
While pears plump with laughter, reaching the sky.

Carrots in rows, doing the twist,
Turnips hold hands, they can't resist.
A bountiful harvest, a field of delight,
Nature's jesters, all day and night.

Cherished Sunshine

Once a squirrel wore shades, quite the sight,
Chasing shadows – oh, what a flight!
He danced on the grass, in a cheeky display,
With acorns as maracas, he'd sway all day.

The flowers giggled, their petals aflutter,
As bees joined the party, buzzing like butter.
A cloud in the shape of a clown popped by,
And everyone wondered, 'Is it time to fly?'

The Tapestry of Cheer

In the kitchen, a cat made a mess,
Whiskers covered in flour, oh, what a dress!
The dog tried to help, with a wag and a spin,
But tripped over tea towels, ending with a grin.

The toaster shot toast as if on a spree,
While chairs held a meeting on who'd spill tea.
A light bulb flickered, joining the banter,
A raucous assembly, to laugh and to canter.

Nectar of the Heart

A penguin in flip-flops, so cool and so bright,
Slide on the ice, oh what a delight!
He dipped into puddles, making big splashes,
While fish gave high-fives, in rainbowed flashes.

A seal with a trumpet played tunes of the deep,
While seagulls formed choirs, in rhythm they leap.
What a wondrous concert, the ocean was grand,
Each wave held the laughter, all part of the band.

Moments of Marvel

In the park, a parade of squirrels went by,
In tiny top hats, they danced towards the sky.
A raccoon in a tux gave a wink and a spin,
As picnickers cheered, letting the fun begin.

A butterfly juggled, with grace and with flair,
While ants brought the snacks, quite the gourmet affair.
When the sun dipped low, they all danced as one,
And under the stars, the laughter was spun.

The Gift of Now

The toaster popped with pride,
As bread did dance and glide.
Jam flew high, quite a show,
Breakfast battles, oh what a flow!

Kids in capes, defy the lawn,
Superheroes at the dawn.
Flying frisbees, laughter loud,
In our chaos, we are proud!

The dog chased shadows, spry and quick,
Round and round, what a trick!
Grass stains, giggles, muddy shoes,
Today's a treasure we won't lose!

Moments of Pure Bliss

A squirrel steals a peanut treat,
Panic hops, oh, what a feat!
With every leap, we share a grin,
Nature's show, let the fun begin!

Tickled by the summer breeze,
We run around, as we please.
Water balloons fly, splashes fly,
Laughter erupts, oh my, oh my!

Ice cream drips on tiny hands,
Sticky joys, sweet demands.
The sun smiles down, a golden cheer,
We dance and play, nothing to fear!

Savoring the Present

In the kitchen, chaos reigns,
Sticky fingers, spilled champagne.
Cookies burn, but who could care?
Laughter mingles in the air!

A dance-off breaks the dull routine,
Moves so silly, sights unseen.
With every twirl, we bump and slide,
In our madness, we take pride!

When dinner's served, the cat jumps high,
Chasing pasta like it's a spy.
We feast, we shout, joy on the table,
In this moment, we are able!

Heartfelt Serenade

Some days we sing, others we snore,
With off-key notes, what's in store?
A serenade from the toilet seat,
Dad's concert proves life can't be beat!

Socks and sandals, fashion's clash,
Uncle Joe makes a joyful splash.
Twirling rounds of silly guffaws,
We capture moments, earn applause!

In this dance of misfit cheer,
We hug 'til smiles outshine the fear.
As time flies, we hold it tight,
These funny scraps, our pure delight!

The Dance of Delight

In a world of wiggles and jigs,
The cats wear hats and dance like pigs.
The dogs are twirling, tails on fire,
As squirrels play drums, oh how they aspire.

Chickens cluck with a funky beat,
Doing the cha-cha, oh what a feat!
The moon is laughing, stars join in,
As everyone spins like they've got a twin.

A snail in shades slides down a hill,
Boogying to jazz, he's got the thrill.
With every step, the grass does sing,
Who knew a garden could be this bling?

Come join this party, oh don't be shy,
Wear your best bow tie, let's reach the sky!
With laughter echoing and feet that fly,
We'll dance until the cupcakes run dry!

Bounty of Bliss

A table set with pies galore,
Peach, cherry, and there's one more.
Tomatoes wearing tiny hats,
Sipping juice with silly sprats.

The waiter's a dog, wheeling a cart,
With taco towers to warm your heart.
Cookies giggle, icing grins,
As jellybeans do cartwheels and spins.

Carrots dance with little shoes,
Playing hopscotch, spreading the news.
The pumpkins laugh, their smiles wide,
In this patch, joy won't hide.

Join the feast, bring your flare,
With goofy faces, let's please the air.
Every bite's a silly prank,
In this bliss, let's fill our tank!

Effervescent Echoes

Bubbles rise in fizzy cheer,
A soda stream of giggles near.
Cupcakes bounce on a trampoline,
Whipping up a frosted scene.

Jellybeans juggle in a line,
While gummies waltz, oh how they shine.
Fizzy drinks burst with a pop,
As laughter echoes, we can't stop.

Balloons join in, floating around,
Wiggling to a merry sound.
Ice cream cones with hats on top,
Spin like tops that never drop.

As confetti rains from the sky,
A sweet parade just passing by.
With every sip our spirits soar,
In bubbles bright, we all explore!

Sweetness in the Air

Cotton candy clouds fluff the sky,
While sugar ants march, oh my, oh my!
Lollipops sway like trees in dance,
As chocolate rivers give us a chance.

Frogs in bow ties croak out a tune,
Playing on leaves beneath the moon.
The butterflies twirl with sprinkles bright,
Creating a scene that's pure delight.

Marshmallow puffs float in the breeze,
Tickling noses with whimsical ease.
A gummy bear leads a parade,
Through candy lanes where dreams are made.

So come on down, grab some flair,
Join the fun, it's everywhere!
In this world of sweets, let's declare,
Life's a hoot, filled with flair!

Vibrant Mirth

Laughter bubbles like a soda,
Tickles hidden in a beanbag,
Silly socks on dancing feet,
Where every tumble is a brag.

Jellybeans on every tree,
Flying kites with socks for tails,
Puppies dressed as grandmas sing,
And squirrels trade their nuts for snails.

Balloons that float and tease the sky,
A cake that wobbles like a frog,
Whiskers twitch on every grin,
As giggles leap from every log.

In a world where silly reigns,
With slippy slides and lots of cheer,
Frogs that wear a bowler hat,
And merry hearts fill every sphere.

Fields of Glee

Dancing daisies in a breeze,
Twirling hats that fly like dreams,
Chasing shadows, skip and hop,
Over puddles, laughter beams.

Caterpillars wiggle wands,
Spinning tales of cheese and mirth,
While crickets play a funky tune,
And frogs proclaim the joy of earth.

Bouncy castles in the sun,
With squeaky shoes on every tree,
A parade of giggling gnomes,
Leaps of joy for all to see.

In fields of glee, where fun runs wild,
With magical sprinkles in the air,
Every moment's an adventure,
And hearts burst free beyond compare.

Overflowing Wonders

Pickles wearing tiny hats,
Mushrooms dancing on a log,
Zany owls with googly eyes,
Script their tales in fluffy fog.

Chocolate rivers full of cheer,
While marshmallows float like boats,
The sun winks down with a giggle,
And clouds wear funny little coats.

Jumping jellies in a race,
Pairing socks with shoes that squeak,
Every moment is a treat,
With surprises every week.

In this land of bouncing dreams,
Where whimsy reigns and joys collide,
Every corner filled with laughs,
Adventures wait, let's joyfully ride.

Luminous Bliss

Glow worms throw a disco party,
As gnomes try their dance moves too,
Bouncing on a trampoline,
With pies that sing a silly tune.

Rainbows sprout from every tree,
Where giggles make the flowers bloom,
Cats pretend to be ballet stars,
While dogs create a dancing room.

Taffy rivers twist and twirl,
As chocolate bunnies hop around,
In this land of funny sights,
Every smile is profound.

So come and join this merry spree,
Where joy shines bright in every glance,
With friends and laughter all around,
Life's just one delightful dance.

Warmth in Every Breath

My coffee's hot, it wakes me up,
Like sunburned toast in a butter cup.
Laughing at socks that do not match,
With every sip, I start to hatch.

The toast pops up, a graceful leap,
Like a kangaroo, it makes me weep.
I giggle at my cereal dance,
Each flake a partner in whims of chance.

The cat looks up, pretends to know,
How joy can make a heart aglow.
Chasing dust motes like tiny stars,
In my living room, there's no need for bars.

So here's my heart, in laughter's thrall,
With each small moment, I stand tall.
Life's silly charm is hard to miss,
Embracing chaos, and sealing with a kiss.

Illumination of the Soul

The lightbulb flickers, then shines bright,
Like goofy faces in morning's sight.
I trip on air, a clumsy ballet,
Yet happiness chases worries away.

My socks are stripes, my shirt's a hue,
Of colors mixed, like a playful zoo.
Dancing with dust bunnies in the hall,
Every tumble, a reason to sprawl.

I wear my hat, it's far too tight,
But who cares? I feel just right!
A rubber chicken's my trusty friend,
Together we laugh, around every bend.

Like sunflowers twirling, in winds that blow,
Silly moments, they help me grow.
The light within, it shines so clear,
Funny faces, the best souvenir.

Dance of the Seasons

Spring sneezes blooms that shimmer bright,
While winter's cold is purely light.
Autumn's leaves do a wiggly show,
Each one dropping, in a laughing flow.

Summer sun is a clumsy friend,
Every sunscreen dab's a giggle send.
We run from storms with umbrellas wide,
Like penguins sliding down a slide.

Time hops about, a curious prank,
In silly shoes, we give a hank.
Let's twirl beneath the starry dome,
With every season, we find our home.

So let's leap and bound, embrace the jest,
In each tick of time, may we feel blessed.
With nature's giggle, let's unwind,
In this dance of seasons, joy's what we find.

Unfolding Happiness

The paper crane takes to the air,
Like laughter fluffs floating everywhere.
In a folding chair, I take a seat,
With comfy socks and my favorite beat.

The popcorn pops with a joyful cheer,
Each kernel's dance is a laugh to hear.
I spill some soda, it bubbles and fizzes,
Like my giggles after silly quizzes.

The doodles I make, they jump and play,
Each squiggly line finds a way to stay.
In every mishap, there's room to grin,
For happiness lives where fun begins.

So let us unfold these moments bright,
With goofy smiles, and hearts so light.
In every hiccup, twist, or bend,
We find the joy that'll never end.

Luminous Pathways

Bright lights dance across the street,
Squirrel in sunglasses, oh so neat.
Pizza in hand, I take a stride,
Laughing at shadows, there's joy inside.

Cats in top hats, what a sight,
Moonbeams giggle, oh so light.
Skip with ducks, they quack a song,
Join their parade, it won't be long.

Lemons on trees, oh what a tease,
Juggling wild socks, just as you please.
Laughter bubbles, a fizzy spree,
Find me dancing, so carefree.

Tickling clouds with fluffy fingers,
In a world where fun just lingers.
Hold your breath while you twirl away,
Chasing rainbows, all night and day.

Wind of Contentment

Breezy whispers tickle my ear,
As I wander without a fear.
Whimsical hats fly up high,
Giggling goats cheerfully sigh.

In the meadow, flowers sway,
Dancing with bees who laugh and play.
Kites in the sky, a colorful fleet,
Each fluttering tail sounds a beat.

Pies cooling on windowsills,
Inviting scents that give me thrills.
I trip over my own two shoes,
And land in a puddle - oh, such blues!

With each step, a silly tune,
A jolly jig beneath the moon.
Wind in my hair, I frolic and spin,
This merry journey, let's begin!

Dreams Awash in Color

Paint the sky in polka dots,
Dancing unicorns, oh what a plot!
Rainbow sprinkles on each tree,
Giggles erupt in pure glee.

Jumping puddles, splashes fly,
With a bubble wand, I soar high.
Cakes that sing a happy tune,
Under the light of a chocolate moon.

Hats that float on clouds so round,
Each giggle makes a funny sound.
Imaginary friends high-five,
In this silly world, we thrive.

Swirling stars, jump up and down,
Painted toes twirl, wear a crown.
Wishing wells that chuckle too,
In dreams so bright, let's sail on through.

Heartstrings in Harmony

Strumming joy on guitar strings,
Laughter flies with the happiness it brings.
Potatoes wearing tiny shoes,
Every step a giggling muse.

Silly faces stuck in the trees,
Chasing squirrels as they tease.
Marshmallow clouds, soft and fluffy,
Jumps so high, it feels so guffy.

Balloons that float out of sight,
With a wink they say, "What a night!"
Giggling every step we take,
A journey filled with twists to make.

Side by side, we dance and spin,
Heartstrings tugging, let the fun begin.
Laughing till our bellies ache,
In harmony, the world we make!

Ecstasy in Bloom

In the garden where giggles grow,
Sunflowers dance, putting on a show.
Bumblebees buzz, taking their course,
While daisies wink with a hint of force.

A pumpkin wore a silly grin,
Bragging of the fun within.
The tomatoes threw a juicy bash,
As carrots tangoed in a flash.

Marigolds sport hats of glee,
Twirling like they're at a spree.
Lettuce laughs as rabbits peek,
While seedlings joke, it's all quite chic.

With every bloom, a chuckle loud,
And everyone sings, feeling proud.
So come along, don't miss the scene,
In this garden, life's a dream!

Joyful Journeys

Pack your bags with laughter bright,
An adventure set, oh what a sight!
Bouncing trains and planes that zoom,
Every stop, a giggle room.

Maps that lead to ice cream lands,
Meeting friends in funny bands.
Every corner hides a pun,
Where sunshine plays and jokes run.

Snorkeling with fish in hats,
Monkeying around with silly chats.
At sunset, we'll paint the shore,
With tickles and belly laughs galore.

So join the ride, don't be late,
Adventure awaits, it's really great!
With joy in every twist and turn,
No dull moment, just fun to earn!

A Symphony of Light

The sun breaks in with a jolly grin,
While shadows dance, hoping to win.
A chorus of colors starts to play,
In a symphonic prank, come what may.

Clouds play hide and seek on cue,
Each one wearing a silly shoe.
Rainbows leap across the sky,
Tickling everyone passing by.

Glowing stars become the band,
While moons tell tales, oh so grand.
Every twinkle has a joke to share,
Making night feel light as air.

In this dazzling, bright delight,
Laughter rings throughout the night.
Join the fun, dance without fright,
In the harmony of sheer delight.

Cornucopia of Cheer

A basket brimming with giggles bright,
Filled with fruits of pure delight.
Bananas smile, and apples sing,
In a fruity party, it's quite the fling.

Peppers jest and carrots prance,
While berries sway in a playful dance.
Join in, what's that? A grape on a roll!
Cracking jokes until they stroll.

In the market, everyone cheers,
As melons juggle through the years.
Slices of laughter served on plates,
Each bite taken, happiness rates.

So grab a fruit, share a laugh,
And let the joy fill up your path.
In this cornucopia, life feels fine,
With every taste, let your grin shine!

Pathways to Bliss

Walking down a silly street,
Where every step's a dancing beat.
Socks mismatched, hair a fright,
Laughter echoing, pure delight.

Chasing squirrels, what a sight,
They steal my sandwich, quick as light.
The world's a stage, I'm the clown,
Wearing joy like a crown.

Pies that fly, and hats that sing,
Life's a circus, do your thing!
With every slip, a hearty cheer,
Who knew bliss was so near?

So here I skip, no cares in tow,
On pathways paved with giggles, oh!
A happy dance, I'll take the lead,
In this madness, I am freed.

Sparkling Moments

Bubbles float like silly dreams,
Chasing laughter, bursting seams.
With squeaky toys and silly hats,
I laugh at birds who steal my snacks.

Sipping juice, it slips my grip,
All over me, what a trip!
My friends all laugh, they can't resist,
A juicy hug, a splashy twist.

The sun's a ball, we're dogs at play,
Rolling in grass on a silly day.
A kite takes flight, we chase it high,
In moments like these, we learn to fly.

Sparkling time, what a tease,
With giggles swaying in the breeze.
These little joys, they fill my heart,
In every laugh, there's magic's art.

The Sweetness of Us

You bring the sugar, I bring the spice,
Together we're a recipe so nice.
Dancing in kitchens, we flour the floor,
A pinch of laughter, and then some more.

Cookies burn, but our smiles shine,
A kitchen chaos, all is divine.
With chocolate chips all over our face,
We'll eat dessert at a breakneck pace.

Your jokes are silly, my puns are grand,
In this crazy partnership, we take a stand.
With every giggle that fills the room,
We make a garden of joyous bloom.

The world's a sweet shop, all our own,
With a sprinkle of humor, we've brightly grown.
Every moment shared, a sugar rush,
Together we thrive in this joyful hush.

Waves of Contentment

Surfing on laughter, riding the waves,
Sliding on sunshine, oh how it saves!
Flip-flops flying, hats take flight,
In a goofy drift, everything's right.

Sand in my toes, a seagull's song,
Making silly castles, it won't be long.
With every splash, a giggle erupts,
Joy in the ocean, this life interrupts.

A towel wraps tight, we're tangled up,
Sharing stories over a coconut cup.
Waves crash down with the lightest smirk,
In this salty joy, we both lurk.

So let's dance among the waves so high,
Under a sun painted bright in the sky.
Here's to the moments, carefree and grand,
In these waves of delight, we truly stand.

Lush Gardens of Gaiety

In the garden, gnomes take flight,
Dancing under the moonlight bright.
Flowers giggle, roots do cheer,
Bumblebees waltz, no sign of fear.

Jumpy rabbits in silly hats,
Join the fun with silly spats.
Petunias talk, tulips tease,
Nature's laughter in the breeze.

Sunflowers sway with carefree flair,
Talking secrets, who knows where?
Butterflies, in makeup bold,
Sing sweet stories never told.

At dusk, the crickets clam and croak,
Laughing loud as each bird folk.
In this place, joy bursts like fries,
With every chortle, the humor flies.

Bursting with Light

A toaster pops, the bread takes flight,
Landing butter-side up, what a sight!
Coffee's brewing, steam's a show,
Mug's smiling wide from head to toe.

Socks mismatch, oh what a trend,
A cat in pajamas, who could pretend?
Giggling clouds, they can't stay still,
Rain decides to dance, oh what a thrill!

Balloons float with a yoyo face,
Juggling pies in a silly race.
Chickens cluck in a tap routine,
All of laughter's cast, the scene!

In the sun, old chairs have chats,
While squirrels plan with acorn hats.
In moments brief, we find the light,
Life's a jest, embraced with delight.

A Symphony of Smiles

Frogs on logs sing harmony,
While crickets join, a jubilee.
With every note, the flowers sway,
As laughter blooms throughout the day.

The sun sets down, a goofy grin,
Reflecting joy from deep within.
Tiny ants parade in line,
With each tiny step, they create a sign.

A rainbow spills like candy dreams,
Ice cream cones, or so it seems.
Wobbly laughter fills the trees,
As breezes tickle leaves with ease.

With every laugh, the world spins round,
In this tune, no frowns are found.
From silly hats to ticklish feet,
Life's a party — oh what a treat!

The Essence of Elation

In the kitchen, pots do clash,
Mixing joy in a bubbly splash.
Cookies whistle with a cheeky tease,
Flour dances like a playful breeze.

Puppies prance in circles wide,
Chasing tails, they slip and slide.
Squeaky toys make a happy sound,
Echoing giggles all around.

Kites soar high, like eagles bright,
In a contest of silly flight.
Fingers stick to candy sweet,
As friends gather for the treat.

Jokes fly like feathers on the ground,
In this joy, pure bliss is found.
So raise a cheer, let out a roar,
For every moment opens a door!

Echoes of Exuberance

Laughter erupts like popcorn in air,
Giggles ignite, with no need to care.
Chasing each other, a whimsical race,
Grins stretched wide, we're in our own space.

Dancing with shadows, we twirl and we spin,
Mirth-filled chaos, oh where to begin?
Tickles and jests, the world's our own stage,
We're clowning around, let's pop up a page.

Life's little quirks, like pie in the face,
Sprinkle some joy, we're in our own place.
Jokes in the air, like bubbles, they rise,
Puns packed with laughter, oh what a surprise!

In the garden of giggles, we plant all our seeds,
Water with chuckles, it's all that one needs.
Watch them bloom brightly, like fireworks bold,
Echoes of laughter, our treasures unfold.

Elixir of Laughter

A spark in the air, we weave silly tales,
Jumping on clouds, like a ship that just sails.
Bottles of humor, we've swirled up a mix,
Stirring up laughter, come join in the fix.

Lemonade skies filled with popsicle dreams,
Juggling the joy, bursting at the seams.
Guffaws in the kitchen, we fry up our words,
Cackles that flitter like winged, happy birds.

Silly hats on, we skip down the street,
Bananas and giggles, a quirky old treat.
Frolicking freely, we bounce like mad peas,
Wiggles and wobbles, a laugh at degrees.

Wine made of chuckles, we sip and we share,
A toast to the jesters, with humor to spare.
Pouring out sunshine, our glasses held high,
Together we sparkle, we're better, oh my!

Cherished Encounters

Meeting at sunup, it's giggles galore,
High-fives and winks as we knock on the door.
Crazy stories tumble from voices so bright,
Each moment a spark, igniting the light.

In a whirl of laughter, we chase silly dreams,
Building old castles as friendship redeems.
Snagging the seconds, with tickles and pranks,
Shaking up fate with our laughter-filled flanks.

Socks worn like hats, we strut through the park,
Dancing with shadows, igniting the spark.
Meeting the moments with grins ear to ear,
Stories to tell, like our own special cheer.

Chasing the sunset, we run hand in hand,
Crafting our joys, a whimsical band.
Cheers echo loudly, our bonds ever strong,
In cherished encounters, we find where we belong.

Symphony of Sunshine

A clatter of giggles sets the mood for the day,
Brass bands of chuckles, come join in the play.
We're marching with joy, like a parade in the sun,
Life's quirky moments, it's all just for fun.

Tickling piano keys, laughter's a sound,
Saxophone sighs as the giggles abound.
Comedic crescendos in a jitterbug flight,
Swinging through sunshine, we dance with delight.

The drums thrum with mischief, a beat that we keep,
Twirling like dervishes, into giggles we leap.
Funny little dances, each note feels so right,
In this symphony crafted, joy takes to flight.

With harmonies bursting, our spirits entwined,
We pluck at the strings that connect heart and mind.
Let the melody soar, with each laugh and cheer,
In our symphony of sunshine, the world disappears.

Splendor in Simplicity

Sunshine spills on my head,
Like a pancake, but instead.
Squirrels dance in the yard,
While I trip on a discarded card.

Lemonade spills on my shoe,
What a day to start anew.
Birds chirp a silly tune,
I laugh and sing to the moon.

A butterfly does a flip,
While I take a clumsy sip.
Life's a mess and that's alright,
With giggles flying in pure delight.

So let the grass tickle my toes,
As the world spins on, and laughter grows.
In simple moments formed by chance,
I find joy in this goofy dance.

Abundant Smiles

A clown slipped on a banana peel,
What a sight, almost surreal!
Laughter bubbles like hot stew,
And I can't help but join in too.

Every giggle's like a spark,
Turning the mundane into art.
With silly faces and big grins,
We act like kids and let joy win.

The dog in a goofy hat,
Chasing its tail, oh imagine that!
Tickled by the world we roam,
In these smiles, we feel at home.

Let's jump in puddles, splash so loud,
Join the chaos; let's be proud.
With every chuckle, hearts align,
In the abundance of laughter, we shine.

Celebration of the Day

Wake up to the sun's big smile,
A dance-off with my cat, worth the while.
Breakfast? Oh, a cookie might do,
Who needs veggies? Not me, it's true.

The neighbor's music, loud and bright,
Weird lyrics make the morning light.
Dancing socks upon the floor,
Who knew chores could bring such a roar?

A toast with juice, I make a cheer,
To funny moments drawing near.
With hats askew and shirts inside out,
We celebrate with twirls and a shout.

The sun dips low, but wait, oh no!
Grass stains on my knees steal the show.
As night falls, laughter fills the air,
All our silly antics, too good to bear.

Nature's Sweet Embrace

In the park, the flowers speak,
Yelling jokes from the tiny creek.
A caterpillar gives a wink,
While I laugh and spill my drink.

Sun rays tickle my nose,
As the big old oak tree doze.
Butterflies in a funny race,
Dance around with silly grace.

The ants march like a parade,
With tiny hats, their grand charade.
Clouds giggle, shaping a bear,
While I try to find him up there.

Nature's laughter fills the air,
A joyful script, no need for flair.
In this adult circus of green,
Ridiculous fun is what we glean.

Euphoria in Every Step

Skip like a frog down the lane,
Dance with a goat—oh, what a gain!
Wiggle your toes, let laughter erupt,
A pie in the face? Yup, we'll erupt!

Socks and sandals, a fashion faux pas,
But who cares? We're laughing with glee, ha-ha!
Jump in the puddles, splash with cheer,
Life's just a joke, let's laugh without fear!

A slip on the banana, oh what a sight,
But land with a grin, the future's so bright!
Wet dog shakes, and a sprinkle of mud,
Giggles arise as we dance in the flood!

So grab your friends, let's run and then play,
In our silly shoes, let's enjoy the day!
Every step, a delight, every turn, a jest,
Time flies with fun—oh, we're truly blessed!

Canvas of Glee

Paint the world with colors so bright,
Splashes of joy, what a wonderful sight!
Every stroke a chuckle, every hue a shout,
A masterpiece born from giggles and clouts!

A brush in my hand, but wait, what's that?
An oversplash of orange—now I'm a cat!
Paws on the canvas, a funny display,
Who knew that art could get so cliché?

Friends join the fun, with paint on our face,
We'll create a mural, a riotous space!
Each smeared fingerprint tells a tale of our glee,
A canvas so wild, it's a sight to see!

So dip in the colors, let laughter ignite,
In this silly studio, everything's right!
Together we'll giggle, together we'll sing,
Creating a joy that only art can bring!

Gratitude in Bloom

A garden of chuckles sprouts flowers galore,
Bumblebees buzzing, but wait—they're hardcore!
Stinging my jokes with a hum and a whirl,
But hey, what's that? Just doing a twirl!

Blooming with thanks for the puns and the quirks,
Sunflowers nodding at all of life's perks!
A toad jumps out, "Hop on this ride!"
Grateful for moments that can't be denied!

Daisies come out for a picnic of laughs,
Join in the fun with field-mushroom staffs!
Twirls in the daisies, wind combs through hair,
Joyful abundance is floating in the air!

So toast to the blooms, the silly and spry,
With gratitude growing, we'll reach for the sky!
Each giggle, a petal, each laugh, a sweet tune,
In this garden of goofiness, we happily swoon!

Mirthful Moments

Oh, what a day for a jolly good laugh,
Chasing a chicken can't be half bad!
Rolling on grass with a watermelon slice,
Turn on the fun—let's roll the dice!

Knock-knock, who's there? It's a dad joke parade,
With punchlines and giggles, we're never delayed!
Falling off chairs? It's all in the game,
In this mirthful dance, we're all kinda lame!

Let's juggle some lemons while wearing a hat,
A slip of a foot, then splat!—just like that!
But laughter's the remedy, brightens the day,
In this circus of life, we'll tumble and play!

So here's to the moments, the silly and wacky,
Together we'll shine, never feeling tacky!
In this joyful embrace, where laughter roams free,
Let's celebrate life, oh, just you and me!

Feast of Heartstrings

A plate full of giggles, a slice of delight,
We dance with our shadows, in dreams of the night.
With chocolate-dipped pickles and jellybean pie,
We feast on absurdity, oh me, oh my!

Laughter is seasoning, we sprinkle it here,
While juggling cantaloupes brings everyone cheer.
The table's a circus, oh what a grand view,
In this banquet of folly, we savor the hue.

Each joke is a morsel, we chew and we chew,
Spinning tales of blunders, with whimsy to strew.
The bread rolls are bouncing, the butter's a star,
In this feast of heartstrings, we laugh near and far.

So grab a light-hearted, and join in the fun,
With each silly quip, we revel as one.
For joy's not a matter of where it's placed,
But found in the giggles, oh what a taste!

Jubilant Encounters

Upon the bright sidewalk, a tumble, a trip,
My coffee does somersaults, as I lose my grip.
The passerby chuckles, we share a quick grin,
In this odd little world, we all try to win.

Two puppies are wrestling, a cat joins the fray,
Canines and felines in their foolish play.
The park is a stage for a comedic scene,
And laughter erupts like a soda can's sheen.

A man in a hat that's far too big,
Tries to catch dreams while he does a jig.
Each twirl brings a giggle, each leap brings a cheer,
In jubilant encounters, all mischief is clear.

So here's to the moments, all quirky and bright,
Where strangers are friends, and the world feels just right.

Let's toast with our laughter, let's dance through the day,
In this joyous confusion, we'll find our own way!

Elysian Echoes

In a field of daisies, a herd of pink cows,
They moo in a rhythm, like jazz from the clouds.
Each step is a melody, a note in the breeze,
As flowers do pirouettes, untying their leaves.

A squirrel with a top hat conducts from a log,
While bunnies in bow ties applaud in the fog.
The moon winks a secret, the stars play along,
In this riot of colors, we hum the right song.

A rainbow bursts forth, it slips on a slide,
With giggles and snickers, it takes quite a ride.
The sun wears a tuxedo, the clouds are all dressed,
In this elysian haven, we feel truly blessed.

So let's join this chorus, this whimsical spree,
In echoes of laughter, we find the key.
With our hearts in the sky, we dance through each hour,
In this bright tapestry, life's a hilarious flower!

Chasing Sparkles

In the attic I found them, my childhood old beads,
A treasure of chuckles from fanciful deeds.
I strung them on laughter, each color a joke,
As sparkles of joy from the past gently spoke.

A dance party starts with my vintage old toys,
They shimmy and shake with the utmost poise.
Each step is a riddle, a hint at the game,
With giggles and wiggles, it's all quite the same.

In the garden of whimsy, we chase after light,
Where daisies debate if a cat's really bright.
With each tiny glimmer, we twirl and we spin,
Chasing sparkles of laughter, where fun does begin.

So gather your chuckles, let's make them our own,
In this merry parade, we'll never feel lone.
Through giggles and sparkles, our spirits will soar,
In this chase of delight, we'll always want more!

Radiant Heartbeats

In the garden where laughter blooms,
Flowers dance like tiny loons.
Each giggle tickles, bright and sweet,
A waltz of joy, no chance to cheat.

Bumblebees buzz with a cheeky grin,
Painting the air, spin to win.
Petals spin like a silly hat,
In this world, where fun is at.

Squirrels juggle nuts with flair,
Laughter echoes in the bright air.
With every hop and tiny cheer,
My heart beats funny, loud and clear.

Clouds pirouette in the blue sky,
As if they're laughing, oh my, oh my!
We chase the sun, a playful game,
In this frolic, nothing is tame.

Sun-kissed Whispers

Under the sun with a grin so wide,
Joy sneaks in, like a playful tide.
Tickling toes in the warm grass,
Every moment happens in a flash.

The laughter of kids, a lovely sound,
In every corner, joy is found.
Echoes of giggles in the breeze,
Life's little flukes bring hearts to ease.

Sunny shades pop like confetti,
With candy vibes that feel so petty.
Jumping puddles, a crazy feat,
Each splash is pure laughter, oh so sweet.

Whispers of glee ride on the air,
As if the world has no care.
In this moment, everything's bright,
We dance 'til dark, beneath the light.

Love on the Horizon

From afar, I see a dance unfold,
A spicy tale that never gets old.
In wobbly boats on a fizzy sea,
Laughter sails where hearts run free.

The horizon winks with a quirky glow,
A game of tag, we come and go.
Each sunset wraps the day in cheer,
With silly moments, always near.

Love struts in, a clownish delight,
Twirling hearts in a playful flight.
We build our dreams on sandy shores,
Chasing wishes, always wanting more.

In every giggle, a spark ignites,
As day gives way to starry nights.
We'll laugh till dawn breaks in the sky,
In this funny love, oh me, oh my!

Gentle Ripples of Joy

In the pond where the frogs all croon,
Ripples dance to a silly tune.
Each splashy jump, a giggle parade,
Joy bounces, nothing's delayed.

Cotton candy clouds float above,
Whispers of fun, all things we love.
The sun throws confetti, bright and bold,
While watermelon dreams never get old.

With every tickle from the breeze,
Life unfurls with playful ease.
Wiggly worms in a slimy race,
Laughter sprawls, a fuzzy embrace.

Let's twirl around like dizzy pears,
Celebrating all the silly snares.
In this carnival of bright delight,
Joy ripples softly, day and night.

Thriving in Serenity

In a garden where giggles bloom,
A chicken wears a hat, oh what a loom!
The bees buzz songs, they dance around,
While trees wear smiles, not a frown to be found.

Socks mismatched, a sight to behold,
A squirrel steals nuts, so brave and bold!
Laughter flows like a bubbling brook,
Nature's comedy in every nook!

Frogs on logs, wearing shades of green,
They croak out jokes, quite the unseen!
The sun dons a grin, a cheerful glare,
Together we bask in the playful air.

With friends by the stream, we joke and play,
Catching silliness that flies away.
In this haven, merriment's our art,
In every chuckle, serenity's heart.

Colors of Contentment

In a field of crayons, colors collide,
The grass says 'Hey!', the flowers reply.
A dog in a tutu prances with glee,
The world's a canvas, just wait and see!

Pigs in pink shades, float up to the sky,
While squirrels wear ties, oh my, oh my!
The daisies laugh, the daisies sing,
In this happy land, who needs a king?

Butterflies giggle as they spin and twirl,
With every flap, they cause quite a whirl.
Chasing rainbows, on a whim, they fly,
Creating vivid storms of laughter nigh.

All shades of giggles paint life's delight,
With every chuckle, the day feels bright.
In this art of joy, we splash and smirk,
Colors of happiness, where dreams work.

Exuberant Horizons

A pogo stick race on a sunny slope,
With llamas in shades, no need for hope.
They bounce and yell, in sheer delight,
Even the clouds start giggling in flight.

The wind winks and sings a silly tune,
As rainbows leap like a cartoon.
With every hop, the sky's set ablaze,
Creating a canvas of laughter craze.

Giraffes in bow ties munch on the hay,
While turtles dance like it's their birthday.
Joy shakes the trees, as they giggle in glee,
In this fun-filled world, we're truly free!

So skip along, let your spirits soar,
In the land of giggles, there's always more.
With hearts so light, and spirits in flight,
Horizons of chuckles fill up the night.

Celebrating the Unseen

Invisible hats are quite the trend,
On dogs with no worries, as they pretend.
They strut down the lane in a comical way,
While pigeons applaud with feathers in sway.

A dance party starts with an empty chair,
The music's so loud, you can faintly hear air.
As shadows groove, the moon gives a wink,
In this party of giggles, just stop and think!

The magic of laughter, a tickle unseen,
Festivities bloom in spaces between.
With joy overflowing, we toast with a cheer,
To all of the moments we hold so dear!

Here's to the quirks and the silliness wide,
In the game of life, come take a ride.
With giggles and grins in our hearts so keen,
Together we cherish the joy that's unseen.

The Magic of Togetherness

In the kitchen chaos, pots start to sing,
A dance of spatulas, together they swing.
Flour in the air, a cloud of delight,
Who knew baking cookies was such a sight?

Laughter erupts, as the cat steals a bite,
Jumps on the counter, such a silly fright!
With dough on our hands and smiles all around,
These moments of madness are joyfully found.

The dog joins the fun, with a wagging tail,
Chasing after sprinkles that decorate the trail.
We trip over giggles, a joyful parade,
In this merry circus, no plans are waylaid.

As the sun sets low, we gather in cheer,
Claiming our cupcakes, our smiles sincere.
In the heart of the madness, love is the key,
Together we sparkle, just you wait and see!

Joy Unbound

In pajamas all day, we declare it's a win,
Dance-offs in the living room, let the games begin!
Bouncing on sofas, a trampoline spree,
With a sprinkle of chaos, just how it should be.

Popcorn explosions and movies galore,
Who needs a theater? We've got our own roar!
Couch pillows wiggle, as we make our stand,
In a fortress of laughter, life feels so grand.

A knock at the door, it's the pizza guy,
With a pie and a wink, we let out a sigh.
Sharing cheesy slices, we toast to the fun,
In our silly little world, joy's never done.

The day drifts away, but our spirits don't fade,
With memories made in this silly charade.
So here's to the moments that tickle our heart,
In this quirky adventure, we never depart!

Festive Memories

Decorations are flapping, the tinsel takes flight,
As we wrestle with ornaments, it's quite the sight.
The tree stands tall, then tips with a sneeze,
"Can someone explain this?" we giggle with ease.

Cake frosting fights, who gets the last lick?
A spatula duel, let's see who is quick!
Sprinkles on faces, our sweet little crown,
With each playful moment, the joy knows no bounds.

The lights are all tangled, a festive mishap,
We twist and we turn, it's a grouping of sap!
But no one is fussing, we giggle and sigh,
As the magic of mayhem dances through the sky.

At dusk we gather, with snacks piled high,
Our hearts feel so full, like the clouds up high.
In the whirlwind of colors, we promise to meet,
For more silly memories, it's joy we repeat!

The Melody of Laughter

Tune in to the giggles, a symphony plays,
As we hum silly songs, and dance in a maze.
With a spoon as a mic, we start the show,
Who knew kitchen concerts would steal the glow?

The cat in a hat, steals all of the limelight,
Pausing for a stretch, holding up his delight.
With each roaring chuckle, the rhythm grows strong,
In this upbeat haven, we all sing along.

Spinning in circles, we reach for the sky,
In this waltz of joy, we can't help but fly.
Our hearts beat in sync to a silly refrain,
With laughter as music, we dance in the rain.

As the clock hands slip away, we cherish the vibe,
Each note of our laughter—a precious little tribe.
So let's sing out loud, 'til the stars twirl too,
In a world stitched with giggles, we'll savor the view!

Blossoms of Delight

In a garden of giggles, blooms take flight,
Petals laugh softly, oh what a sight!
Bees wear tiny hats, buzzing with glee,
While daisies do the cha-cha, wild and free.

Sunshine bursts forth in a playful embrace,
Worms do the twist, find their own pace.
Butterflies twirl, chasing after their dreams,
Nature's own circus, bursting with beams.

Whispers of Bliss

Squirrels in comedy, slipping on leaves,
Juggling acorns, they're taking their leaves!
Chirping birds gossip, secrets the trees hold,
Laughter echoes lightly, like stories retold.

The wind plays a tune, a whimsical note,
Dancing through branches on a joyful boat.
Even the rocks chuckle under the sun,
Nature's own giggle, oh, what fun!

Fields of Radiant Smiles

In fields of laughter, where daisies beam,
Cows crack jokes, fulfilling their dream.
Sheep dress in fluff, like clouds in the sky,
While pigs don top hats, oh my, oh my!

The breeze whispers laughter, tickling the air,
Wheat does a jig, with style and flair.
Farmers join in, doing the worm,
In a world so silly, we all affirm.

Sweetness in the Air

Honey drips laughter from a curious hive,
Bees sing sweet tunes, feeling alive.
Cupcakes compete in a frosting race,
With sprinkles as crowns, they embrace the space.

Lollipop trees sway in a candyland trance,
As jellybeans jive in their own little dance.
The world is a circus, oh what a show,
In a land full of sweetness, happiness flows!

Embracing the Sunshine

The sunbeam tickles my nose,
Like a playful puppy that knows.
I dance in my mismatched socks,
While my coffee's stuck in a box.

A bird chirps a tune so absurd,
As if it's just heard a word.
I twirl like a kid on a swing,
Pretending to be a bright, bold king.

My hat flies off, oh what a sight,
Chasing it feels like pure delight.
The flowers nod their heads in glee,
Making a ruckus, just like me.

With sandals that squeak on the floor,
I open my heart and then more.
The sunshine's laughter fills the air,
In this moment, we're free as a bear.

Tapestry of Gratitude

I'm thankful for silly things,
Like waffles with funny blings.
With syrup that dances and spins,
My breakfast is ready to win.

The cat in a hat prances around,
As if it's the king of the town.
I'm grateful for socks that don't match,
And silly doodles that I can sketch.

The coffee spills, oh what a mess,
Yet somehow, it adds to the zest.
Each moment is stitched with delight,
In this tapestry, colors ignite.

To friendship and laughter, I raise,
A toast that will surely amaze.
With giggles that join in a cheer,
Gratitude sparkles, oh so clear.

Uplifted Spirits

I climbed up a hill with a grin,
Hoping to find a wild spin.
A butterfly said, "What's the fuss?"
"Just laughing and teasing, no need to rush!"

The breeze plays tricks on my hair,
Like a mischievous child everywhere.
I'm leaping around like a frog,
Chasing away the heavy fog.

Suddenly, a squirrel stops to stare,
With a nut, it looks quite debonair.
I chuckle and cheer, bring on the fun,
As clouds dance about under the sun.

With each silly step that I take,
I'm learning to wiggle and shake.
Uplifted spirits, oh what a thrill,
Let's dance to the beat of our will!

The Color of Laughter

In a world that's painted in giggles,
Where silliness sparkles and wiggles.
Oh what a hue, bright and alive,
Laughter's the fuel, we thrive and jive.

A rainbow made of chuckles and glee,
Every shade tells a joke, can't you see?
Elephants dancing, oh what a tune,
Underneath the light of a silly moon.

Cartwheeling through puddles of cheer,
Splashing colors that brightly appear.
Each snort and chortle adds to the scene,
Creating a canvas, vivid and keen.

With colors that shine from deep within,
Every laugh, like a spin of a pin.
The world looks brighter, full of surprise,
In laughter's embrace, we all truly rise.

Vibrant Echoes

A squirrel danced, with socks on his feet,
He twirled and spun, oh what a treat!
The sun joined in, with a wink and a grin,
While birds chirped back, 'Come on, let's spin!'

A cat on a skateboard rolled on by,
I laughed so hard, I almost cried.
The flowers giggled, swaying with glee,
And clouds whispered softly, 'Come play with me!'

The wind played tunes with a playful breeze,
While ants in a row marched with such ease.
A rainbow appeared, just for the show,
Saying, "Life's a circus, so let's go!"

Laughter erupted, in colors so bright,
With tickles and chuckles, the world felt right.
Let's dance to the rhythm, with no cares at all,
In this vibrant echo, let's have a ball!

The Art of Happiness

With a paintbrush made of sunshine and glee,
I splashed on the canvas, as happy as can be.
The clouds turned pink, while daisies danced,
And even the snails, in slow motion, pranced.

A cupcake winked, with frosting so bright,
Called out, "Come taste, it's sheer delight!"
The jellybeans giggled, wiggling about,
In a world where happiness was never in doubt.

A frog wore a top hat, croaking a tune,
He jived with the lilies under the moon.
The stars had their own little jig to the beat,
While fireflies flickered, making the night sweet.

Each moment a brushstroke of laughter and fun,
In this masterpiece of joy, we're all just one.
So grab a canvas, let's paint our delight,
In the art of happiness, our hearts take flight!

Pure Moments of Radiance

A goldfish wore goggles, swimming with flair,
Bubbling with giggles, without a care.
The sunlight bounced off the ruffled waves,
As crabs in tuxedos performed little braves.

A flower proclaimed, "I'm a dancing queen!"
While bees did the cha-cha, a sight to be seen.
Butterflies fluttered, throwing confetti,
Saying, "Pure moments, come join the spaghetti!"

With ice cream mountains, and candy rain,
I laughed so hard, I felt no pain.
The sun peeked shy in a playful array,
While penguins in hats skated joyfully away.

Each giggle and chortle, a spark in the air,
These moments of magic, beyond compare.
In a world so grand, with fun as our creed,
Pure moments of radiance, life's sweetest seed!

Joyous Reflections

A mirror smiled back with a curious wink,
As shadows turned silly, as if they could think.
I tripped on my shoes, what a clumsy ballet,
While puddles reflected my splashy display.

A dog in a bowtie chased after a cat,
While rainbows rumbled, "Now, how 'bout that?"
The sun tickled trees, wrapped them in light,
While squirrels debated who'd fly a kite.

A picnic was planned with jelly and jam,
While ants set the table in a fancy glam.
With laughter surrounding, all worries took flight,
In joyous reflections, everything felt right.

So let's dance with shadows, sing to the moon,
Life's quirks are the melody, our hearts are the tune.
With every sweet giggle, our spirits will soar,
In this dance of reflections, let's ask for more!

Sunlit Harmonies

The sun smiles wide, oh what a sight,
Bees buzzing loudly, taking flight.
Flowers giggle, swaying in line,
Dancing with shadows, feeling divine.

Chasing a butterfly, I trip on a shoe,
Falling in laughter, what else can I do?
Grass tickles my toes, oh what a tease,
Nature's chorus sings, bringing me ease.

The clouds play tag, drifting so slow,
I wave like an idiot, just for show.
Sunbeams high-five, casting warm rays,
Each moment is silly, fill me with praise.

Every leaf whispers, secrets in air,
A squirrel grins brightly, without a care.
In this light-hearted, vibrant spree,
Life's little wonders are all I see.

Abundance of Elation

Pies in the window, a sight so grand,
Lemons are laughing, rolling on sand.
Muffins are dancing, in a conga line,
Even burnt toast thinks it can shine.

The milk jug winks as I pour a glass,
Spilling it all, oh what a mass!
Eggs jump in pans, making a fuss,
I swear they're plotting, just to discuss.

Lettuce gets pet, tomatoes get hugs,
Pickles do pirouettes, giving me shrugs.
In this kitchen of quirks, I can't help but grin,
Every spoon's got a tale, a secret within.

Flour clouds swirl, like snow on a peak,
Rolling pins giggle, so fluffy and sleek.
Bakers unite, in a fabulous show,
Creating sweet chaos, as they bake dough.

Bounty of Contentment

Jellybeans jump, in my cheerful cup,
Chocolates whisper, 'Hey, eat me up!'
Cookies are plotting their sugary scheme,
While ice cream dreams melt, like a sweet cream.

A candy parade, with licorice lanes,
Gummy bears giggle, with silly refrains.
Lollipops twirl, in a colorful dance,
While cupcakes smile, giving frosting a chance.

Soda pops fizz, making hats go wild,
Sugar rush giggles, a nostalgic child.
Marshmallows float, in a fluffy sea,
In this world of sweetness, there's joy for me.

Candy corn winks, an autumn delight,
In this sweet chaos, everything feels right.
With sprinkles like stars, on my slice of cake,
Each bite tells a tale, in this joyful wake.

Dance of the Heart

My heart does the salsa, with glee in each beat,
Tap dancing on clouds, oh what a feat!
With each twirl and spin, I feel so alive,
Skipping through raindrops, a graceful dive.

A tango with joy, oh isn't it grand?
Moonbeams are partners, holding my hand.
Feet shuffle softly, gliding with grace,
In this silly bash, I find my place.

Hearts laugh like children, without a care,
Cartwheeling through sunlight, in the open air.
Laughter erupts, like bubbles that gleam,
Life's a jovial dance, a whimsical dream.

So let's twist and twirl, under starry skies,
With rhythm and laughter, let worries fly.
Each heartbeat a song, a playful restart,
Join in the fun, oh, the dance of the heart.